Dr K M A Ahamed Zubair

Luminaries of Excellence, Eminence and Enlightenment

Dr K M A Ahamed Zubair

Luminaries of Excellence, Eminence and Enlightenment

Legacies of Shaikh Makhdoom Abdul Haq Sawi and Moulvi Muhammad Mahdi Wasif

Noor Publishing

Imprint
Any brand names and product names mentioned in this book are subject to trademark, brand or patent protection and are trademarks or registered trademarks of their respective holders. The use of brand names, product names, common names, trade names, product descriptions etc. even without a particular marking in this work is in no way to be construed to mean that such names may be regarded as unrestricted in respect of trademark and brand protection legislation and could thus be used by anyone.

Cover image: www.ingimage.com

Publisher:
Noor Publishing
is a trademark of
Dodo Books Indian Ocean Ltd. and OmniScriptum S.R.L publishing group

120 High Road, East Finchley, London, N2 9ED, United Kingdom
Str. Armeneasca 28/1, office 1, Chisinau MD-2012, Republic of Moldova, Europe
Printed at: see last page
ISBN: 978-620-7-47888-0

Luminaries of Excellence, Eminence and Enlightenment

Legacies of Shaikh Makhdoom Abdul Haq Sawi and Moulvi Muhammad Mahdi Wasif

Dr.K.M.A.Ahamed Zubair

Associate Professor of Arabic, The New College,
Chennai 600 014, India

اللغة العربية تحمل كلمة الله، وروح محمد ﷺ، وسر الإسلام،

This work has been dedicated to the Indian

Islamic Missionaries

Preface

Shaikh Makhdoom Abdul Haq Sawi

In the annals of Sufism, few luminaries shine as brightly as Shaikh Makhdoom Abdul Haq Sawi, whose profound spiritual legacy continues to inspire seekers of truth and wisdom across generations. Born into a time of intellectual fervor and spiritual introspection, Shaikh Makhdoom Abdul Haq Sawi's life traversed the realms of mysticism, scholarship, and profound devotion to God.

Throughout his life, Shaikh Makhdoom Abdul Haq Sawi penned numerous works that elucidated the esoteric dimensions of Islamic thought, particularly within the framework of Sufi philosophy. His writings, characterized by their clarity and depth, served as beacons guiding earnest souls toward a deeper understanding of divine truths and the path to spiritual realization.

In this book, we embark on a journey to explore the multifaceted legacy of Shaikh Makhdoom Abdul Haq Sawi. We delve into his teachings on the Unity of Existence (وحدة الوجود), his interpretations of mystical concepts, and his unwavering adherence to the principles of Shariah alongside the pursuit of spiritual enlightenment. Through meticulous exploration of his life's work and profound insights, we aim to illuminate the path he paved for seekers striving to attain closeness to the Divine.

This book is not merely a biographical sketch but a testament to the enduring relevance of Shaikh Makhdoom Abdul Haq Sawi's teachings in contemporary times. It seeks to resonate with readers who yearn for spiritual fulfillment and seek guidance from the wisdom of Sufi masters who, like Shaikh Makhdoom Abdul Haq Sawi, dedicated their lives to the service of God and humanity.

Join us as we embark on this journey of discovery and enlightenment, uncovering the timeless wisdom and spiritual profundity of Shaikh Makhdoom Abdul Haq Sawi.

Moulvi Muhammad Mahdi Wasif

In the annals of scholarship and literary prowess in the Indian subcontinent, few figures shine as brightly as Moulvi Muhammad Mahdi Wasif. Born in 1217 AH (1802 AD) and passing away in 1290 AH (1873 AD), Wasif traversed an era marked by intellectual ferment, cultural revival, and profound socio-political change. His life, spanning nearly a century, embodies a relentless pursuit of knowledge across languages and disciplines, leaving an indelible mark on Arabic, Persian, and Urdu literature.

This book is a testament to Wasif's multifaceted contributions — as a poet, scholar, educator, and chronicler of his times. Through meticulous research and deep exploration, this volume aims to illuminate the life and achievements of a luminary whose intellectual curiosity knew no bounds. From his formative years studying under distinguished mentors in Hyderabad and Madras to his pivotal role in advancing Arabic and Persian studies among East India Company employees, Wasif's journey unfolds as a saga of dedication and scholarly excellence.

Throughout these pages, readers will encounter Wasif's literary oeuvre, including his acclaimed works such as "Ma'dan-al-Jawahir," "Lulu-e-Manthur," and "Rawza-e-Rizwan," each reflecting his mastery of language and profound insight into diverse cultural traditions. His proficiency extended beyond poetry, encompassing treatises on ethics, translations of classical works, and critical analyses that enriched intellectual discourse during his era.

Beyond his literary pursuits, Wasif's life was intertwined with the socio-political currents of his time. His encounters with fellow poets and scholars, his role in poetic assemblies, and his steadfast commitment to preserving and propagating knowledge offer invaluable insights into the intellectual milieu of 19th-century India.

As we delve into the legacy of Moulvi Muhammad Mahdi Wasif, we embark on a journey not only through the life of a singular scholar but also through a pivotal period in South Asian history. This book endeavors to honor his memory, celebrate his contributions, and inspire future generations to cherish the enduring legacy of one of the region's foremost literary figures.

Dr K M A Ahamed Zubair

Contents

Preface	03-06
Luminaries of Excellence, Eminence and Enlightenment :Legacies of Shaikh Makhdoom Abdul Haq Sawi	07-45
Luminaries of Excellence, Eminence and Enlightenment :Legacies of Moulvi Muhammad Mahdi Wasif	46-73
Conclusion	74-75
Bibliography	76-77

Shaikh Makhdoom Abdul Haq Sawi (died 1165 A.H.)

Shaikh Makhdoom Abdul Haq Sawi was the son of Abdun Nabi Agha, son of Muhammad Makhdoom Agha, son of Ibrahim Adil Shah the first, son of Ismail Shah, son of Yousuf Adil Shah, the originator of the kingdom of Bijapur. Since he came from Turkey with a businessman from Sawa, he was known as a person from Sawa. This designation was later used for his descendants, and thus all the ancestors of Makhdoom Abdul Haq were known as "Sawi."

Shaikh Makhdoom Abdul Haq was born in Bijapur. His mother passed away before he turned seven, and his father also died before he reached maturity. He studied Arabic and Persian under various teachers in Bijapur. Later, he moved to Basmatnagar, in the district of Nizamabad in Hyderabad state. He studied mysticism under the renowned saint Shah Nasiruddin, who admitted him into the Qadriya order. He learned Arabic from Shah Syed Ibrahim Shah Mir. He was very intelligent and had a lovable and pleasing demeanor. His spiritual guide, Shah Nasiruddin, married his daughter to him. Shortly after their marriage, he left for Mecca and Medina, where he lived for three years. There, he had the opportunity to meet and discuss with several scholars from all parts of the world. After returning to India, he toured all the important places in the country, acquiring knowledge, especially in the art of mysticism. Syed Anwarullah writes:

"In the sciences of mysticism and truths, he had perfect mastery. No one could present the truths of these sciences before him and speak on these topics."(Mishkat al-Nubuwwat).

He then moved to Madras at the invitation and encouragement of his teacher Shah Syed Ibrahim Shah Mir. He became the disciple of Khawja Rahmatullah, who was known as the deputy of the Prophet (نائب رسول الله).

Khawja Rahmatullah's father, Khawja Mohammed Alam, belonged to the Naqshbandia order. He came to India from Turan and married a pious lady from Bijapur, who gave birth to Khawja Rahmatullah around 1115 A.H. Unfortunately, his mother passed away when he was a small boy. His father remarried and settled in Belgaum. Khawja Rahmatullah then moved to Kurnool, where his maternal aunt took great care of him and ensured his education. He was deeply interested in theology and mysticism. He was initiated into the order of Syed Ahmad Alawi Burumi, who had come from Hadhramaut and settled in Bijapur. Syed Ahmad traced his mystical lineage to Syed Abdul Qadir Jeelani through:

Syed Abdullah Burumi,

Syed Abdullah Bafaqeeh,

Shaikh Muhammad bin Yousuf,

Shaikh Aminuddin Marwahi,

Shaikh Sirajuddin Umar,

Shaikh Abdul Qadir al-Yamani,

Shaikh Ahmad bin Moosa al-Mashrooi,

Shaikh Abu Bakr bin al-Salami al-Yamani,

Shaikh Ismail bin al-Siddiq al-Jabrati,

Shaikh Muhammad al-Muzjaji al-Yamani,

Shaikh Ismail bin Ibrahim al-Zabidi,

Shaikh Sirajuddin al-Yamani,

Shaikh Muhyuddin Ahmad bin Muhammad al-Asadi,

Shaikh Fakhruddin Abu Muhammad bin Ali bin Yaghnam,

Shaikh Muhammad bin Ahmad al-Asadi,

Shaikh Muhammad bin Abdullah al-Asadi,

Shaikh Abdullah bin Yousuf al-Asadi,

Shaikh Abdullah bin Ali al-Asadi, who was a disciple of Shaikh Abdul Qadir Jeelani.

Khawja Rahmatullah worked for a time in the service of the Faujdar of Kurnool. However, he dedicated much of his time to studying mysticism. He decided to visit Arabia and traveled to Mylapore, Madras, intending to proceed to Mecca via Tellicherry. In Madras, he met Syed Hamid Rifai and joined his order. He then reached Jeddah and Mecca, where he met Syed Ashraf Makki, a saint of the Mujaddidiya order, founded by Shaikh Ahmad Sarhindi (937-1033 A.H.), better known as Mujaddid-e-Alf-e-Thani, the Reviver of the Second Millennium. Syed Ashraf Makki was a disciple of Shah Muhammad Tahir, who was a disciple of Shah Muhammad, who was a disciple of Shah Sharafuddin Muqbili.

Shaikh Makhdoom Abdul Haq lived at Rahmatabad, Nellore, where he was admitted into the Sufi order by Khawja Rahmatullah. He later married Halim Saheba, the daughter of Khawja Rahmatullah, and also took a third wife, Haji Hurmatun Nisa.

Khawja Rahmatullah was a student and disciple of Shaikh Ahmad Sarhindi. He was admitted into Shaikh Adam Binnori's order and observed mystical exercises and prayers with such enthusiasm and fervor that he soon attained the spiritual eminence he desired.

The exact year of Khawja Rahmatullah's pilgrimage to Mecca is not known, but since his religious preceptor Syed Ashraf Makki died on the 29th of Zul Hijja in 1149 A.H., it can be concluded that he visited Mecca at least three years before this date. He lived in the two holy places for three years before leaving for India on a ship from Surat. In Surat, he met Shah Ali Raza Gujarati, who was highly esteemed by scholars and the common people. Shah Ali Raza and his father Shah Muhammad held prominent positions in the Mughal court. Shah Ali Raza was the religious preceptor of Sultan Muizzuddin Shah. When the

Sultan was killed in 1125 A.H. (1713 A.D.), Farrukhsiyar, the succeeding emperor, ordered Shah Ali Raza to come to Delhi from Ahmadabad. Ghaziuddin Firuze Jung, the governor of Gujarat, was one of his faithful adherents and secretly advised him to leave immediately. Shah Ali Raza went to Surat, boarded a ship for Jeddah, and lived in Mecca and Medina for about six years, performing pilgrimages four times during this period. He returned to India after Farrukhsiyar's death in 1132 A.H. (1719 A.D.), and was greeted with great enthusiasm and respect.

Prominent Sufis like Shah Abul Fattah (d. 1165 A.H.), Shah Ghulam Hussain (d. 1176 A.H.), Shah Fazli, the son of Shah Kareemullah Qadri, Shah Ali, and others became his disciples. Shah Ali Raza died on the 10th of Ramadhan, though the year of his death is not known. It is said that he had about 170 accomplished successors (خليفه) who began to preach godhood among the people. Khawja Rahmatullah also joined his order and lived with his master for a few days before returning to Kurnool. However, being a puritan in spirit and behavior, he could not tolerate anything against the explicit orders and commandments of Allah and his Apostle.

Begum, who passed away on the 3rd of Zul Qada 1213 A.H., had thirteen sons and six daughters from his three wives. Their names include Baba Saheb, Muhyuddin Saheb, Haneef Saheb, Ghulam Saheb, and Abu.

He was diligent in his prayers and fasting, strictly adhering to the teachings of the Prophet in all aspects of daily life, and encouraged his followers to do the same. He was critical of those who indulged in extravagance and showiness during marriage ceremonies. He also strongly opposed the practice of carrying the symbolic hands (رنجه) of Imam Hussain, the bier (تابوت), and the standards (اعلام) in processions during the first ten days of Muharram each year. As a result, both Sunni and Shia communities turned against him, with few supporting his cause.

He moved to Nandyal but faced the same lack of acceptance from his co-religionists. Afterward, he relocated to Cuddapah and then to Sidhout, encountering similar opposition each time. Eventually, he settled in Anasamandar Pettai, about thirty miles west of Nellore. According to a letter in "Rugat-e-Amiri" by Syed Ameeruddin Ali of Udayagiri, addressed to Hafiz Nasir, Khawja Rahmatullah moved to Anasamandar Pettai at the invitation of Syed Ameeruddin Ali's father and uncle, who were the Jagirdars of Udayagiri. Ameeruddin Ali died in 1207 A.H. and was buried in Nayadupettai.

Syed Abdul Qadir Khan (son of Syed Badruddin, grandson of Syed Mustafa, great-grandson of Syed Ibadullah) and other family members joined Khawja Rahmatullah's order. His reputation grew, attracting learned men like Shaikh Fakhruddin Mehkari Naiti (d. 1143 A.H.),

Syed Shah Abul Hasan Qurbi of Vellore (d. 1182 A.H.), and Shaikh Makhdoom Abdul Haq Sawi of Madras (d. 1165 A.H.) as his disciples. Nawab Mohammad Ali Walajah also sought his prayers and blessings. Khawja Rahmatullah occasionally visited Madras and other locations, becoming a beloved and revered figure throughout the southern region. Many people enthusiastically associated themselves with his order.

The village of Anasamandar Pettai was renamed Rahmatabad. He purchased five villages at a nominal price, and Abdul Qadir Khan donated the villages of Velukula-gunta and Kommalammapadu to him.

He was likely the Jagirdar of Udayagiri. In 1176 A.H., he constructed a mosque, as evidenced by the following chronogram inscribed on a black stone placed on the front wall:

ز طغرا سكه زد من رحمة الله به هر كس را توئى اميد رحمت

كه هاتف گفت در تاريخ مسجد نمودند مسجد اقصى رحمة الله

۱۱۷٦ ه

He dedicated the remainder of his life to preaching and guiding his students and followers. He authored a short Persian book titled "Tanbeeh-al-Anam fiz Zajri an it Tabuti wal Alam" (تنبيه الانام في الزجر عن التابوت والاعلام), which is divided into an introduction (مقدمه), three chapters (تنبيه), and an epilogue (خاتمه). The sections are as follows:

15

مقدمه: On the definition of innovation.

تنبیه اول: On proving the innovativeness of erecting standards and biers.

تنبیه ثانی: On explaining several major sins linked to these innovations.

تنبیه ثالث: On discussing some other innovations related to the standards.

خاتمه: On the virtues of the pure family of the Prophet.

A manuscript copy of this book can be found in the library of Diwan Saheb in Madras.

Additionally, two other tracts written in Dakani, known as "Risala-e-Bidat" (رساله بدعت) and "Irshad Nama" (ارشاد نامه), are still in existence. These works also address the topic of longstanding innovations (بدعات) and emphasize the need to eliminate them from the Muslim community.

He was likely the Jagirdar of Udayagiri. In 1176 A.H., he constructed a mosque, as indicated by the following chronogram inscribed on a black stone in the front wall:

ز طغرا سکه زد من رحمة الله به هر کس را توئی امید رحمت

که هاتف گفت در تاریخ مسجد نمودند مسجد اقصی رحمة الله

"In the name of Rahmatullah, I stamped a seal. You are the hope of mercy for everyone. The divine voice declared in the year of the mosque's construction: 'They established the Aqsa Mosque of Rahmatullah' – 1176 A.H."

He dedicated the remainder of his life to teaching and guiding his students and followers. He wrote a concise book in Persian called "Tanbeeh-al-Anam fiz Zajri an it Tabuti wal Alam" (تنبیه الانام في الزجر عن التابوت والاعلام), which is structured with an introduction, three chapters, and an epilogue. The sections are as follows:

مقدمه در تعریف بدعت

"Introduction: On the definition of innovation."

تنبیه اول در اثبات بدعیت نصب اعلام و تابوت

"First Chapter: On proving the innovativeness of erecting standards and biers."

تنبیه ثانی در بیان کبایر چند که این بدعت قباحت پیوند مفضی بآن است

"Second Chapter: On explaining several major sins associated with these innovations."

تنبیه ثالث در بیان بعضی از بدعت ها که مناسبت تمام به بدعت اعلام دارد

"Third Chapter: On discussing other innovations related to the standards."

خاتمه در ذکر فضایل عترت طاهره

"Epilogue: On the virtues of the pure family of the Prophet."

A manuscript copy of this book is preserved in the library of Diwan Saheb in Madras.

Shaikn Makhdoom Abdul Haq died at Hyderabad on 3rd Rajab 1165 A.H.

Khawja Rahmatullah fell ill while he was a guest of Syed Abdul Qadir Khan, the Jagirdar of Udayagiri. A carbuncle appeared on his cheek which developed further and further and could not be cured by any treatment. Inspite of strong fever and severe pain, he was regularly and punctually attending the five daily congregational prayers. His illness prolonged for about a month. He was requested to appoint a successor خلیفه to him. He said that there was no need to appoint a successor. Some of his sincere students and adherents will take up his cause and support it as desired by him. He breathed his last on Thursday the 25th Rabiul Awwal in the year 1195 A.H after sunset prayer. But the body was brought to Rahmatabad and was laid down at rest in a graveyard on the eastern side of the mosque on which a huge mausoleum of five arches on each side was later on constructed by Nawab Walajah. His wife has also been buried by his side.

It seems Khawja Rahmatullah used to compose poems in Persian also. Three of his verses have been quoted in some of the anthologies. He says:-

از درون خودشناس و کار با گفتار نیست با دل و حدت نظر کر یار ہے اغیار نیست بر
جمالی در کمالی طالب دیدار باش گر شناسی آن جمالت کار با انکار نیست رحمة الله حق
بجوئی از خودی خود دور کن خود نباشی حق نماید حجت و تکرار نیست

His mission progressed and flourished through the efforts of his disciple Moulvi Shah Rafeeuddin Qandhari, who was elected by the people as his successor. He was born at Qandhar a place in Hyderabad state in 1164 A.H. and studied Arabic and Persian under his father

Mohammed Shamsuddin Naqshbandi and other teachers. He was admitted into the order instituted by Khawja Rahmatullah and became a successor to him after his death. He died in 1241 A.H. He is the author of several works like)1(Thamarat-al-Makkiya 2) ثمرات المكيه(Risalah-e-Istilahat-e- Naqshbandiya 3) رساله اصطلاحات نقشبنديه(Risalah-e-Suluk-e-Qadriya Muhammad Asadullah Saheb (d. 3rd Rabi I 1238 A.H.) had six children: Maryam Bee, Shahar Banu, Fatima, Aisha, Fatima, and Saheba.

Shaikh Makhdoom Abdul Haq passed away in Hyderabad on 3rd Rajab 1165 A.H. Khawja Rahmatullah fell ill while staying with Syed Abdul Qadir Khan, the Jagirdar of Udayagiri. He developed a carbuncle on his cheek, which worsened despite various treatments. Despite suffering from severe pain and high fever, he continued to attend the five daily congregational prayers regularly. His illness lasted about a month. When asked to appoint a successor, he stated it was unnecessary, believing his dedicated students and followers would continue his mission. He passed away on Thursday, 25th Rabiul Awwal, 1195 A.H., after the sunset prayer. His body was transported to Rahmatabad and buried in a graveyard on the eastern side of the mosque, where a large mausoleum with five arches on each side was later constructed by Nawab Walajah. His wife was also buried beside him.

Khawja Rahmatullah also composed Persian poetry. Three of his verses are quoted in anthologies:

از درون خودشناس و کار با گفتار نیست

با دل و حدت نظر کر یار ہے اغیار نیست

بر جمالی در کمالی طالب دیدار باش

گر شناسی آن جمالت کار با انکار نیست

"Know yourself from within and don't just rely on words.

With a unified heart, seek your friend, for there are no strangers.

Seek beauty in perfection and be a seeker of vision.

If you recognize that beauty, denial has no place."

رحمۃ اللہ حق بجوئی از خودی خود دور کن

خود نباشی حق نماید حجت و تکرار نیست

"Seek God's mercy; distance yourself from your ego.

If you are not self-centered, the truth will reveal itself without doubt or repetition."

His mission continued to thrive through the efforts of his disciple Moulvi Shah Rafeeuddin Qandhari, chosen by the people as his successor. Born in Qandhar, Hyderabad state, in 1164 A.H., Rafeeuddin studied Arabic and Persian under his father Mohammed Shamsuddin Naqshbandi and other teachers. He joined Khawja Rahmatullah's order and became his successor after his death, passing away in 1241 A.H. He authored several works, including "Thamarat-al-Makkiya," "Risalah-e-Istilahat-e-Naqshbandiya," and "Risalah-e-Suluk-e-Qadriya."

Muhammad Asadullah Saheb (d. 3rd Rabi I 1238 A.H.) had six children: Maryam Bee, Shahar Banu, Fatima, Aisha, Fatima, and Saheba.

Shaikh Makhdoom Abdul Haq passed away in Hyderabad on 3rd Rajab 1165 A.H.

Khawja Rahmatullah fell ill while staying with Syed Abdul Qadir Khan, the Jagirdar of Udayagiri. A carbuncle appeared on his cheek and worsened despite various treatments. Despite severe fever and pain, he diligently attended the five daily congregational prayers. His illness persisted for about a month. When asked to appoint a successor (خليفه), he replied that it was unnecessary; his sincere students and followers would continue his cause as he wished. He passed away on Thursday, 25th Rabiul Awwal, 1195 A.H., after the sunset prayer. His body was transported to Rahmatabad and laid to rest in a graveyard on the eastern side of the mosque. Later, Nawab Walajah constructed a grand mausoleum with five arches on each side. His wife was buried beside him.

Nothing is recorded about his family It is said he married Habeeba Khatun the daughter of the Nawab of Kurnool. There is a reference in تحریك الشفاہ باوصاف والاجاہ 1 Tahreekush Shifah bin Ausaf e Walajah by Nawab Amir-ul-Umara (Died 1203 A.H.) to Mohammad Akbar as the brother-in-law of Khawja Rahmatullah. It is not known whether he married another woman also. Among his children only the name of Halima Khatun is mentioned who was married to Shaikh Makhdoom Abdul Haq Sawi.

Moulana Baqir Agah of Vellore had great faith in the spirituality of Khawja Rahmatullah. He got infuriated when some of the Shias composed a verse giving the date of the death of the Khawja as سگ خبیث a wicked It was one of the causes for starting the bitter controversy between the Sunnis and Shias in 1207, which continued till 1216 A.H., about which we will hear later. Agah composed the following chronogram.

سر اهل یقین وخواجة دین ملاذ و ملجاء هر سالك راه تنش وابسته حكم شریعت دلش از هر مقام و حال آگاه ازیں دار فنا بگذشت و بگذاشت دل احباب را در درد جانگاه بر آمد از صریر خامه فریاد بحق گردید واصل رحمة الله

His body remained in a coffin for six months in the cemetery of Khawja Rahmatullah Khan in Hyderabad. Subsequently, it was transported to Madras and interred in the cemetery at Mylapore, now known by his title, "Dargah Dastageer Sahib Sawi."

Titles of Works:

Risalah-e-Suluk-e-Chishtiya (Chishti Sufi Order Treatise)

Risalah-e-Suluk-e-Qadriya (Qadiri Sufi Order Treatise)

Risalah-e-Suluk-e-Naqshbandiya (Naqshbandi Sufi Order Treatise)

Risalah-e-Masayil-e-Tasawwuf (Treatise on Sufi Issues)

Risalah-e-Kanz-al-Hisab (Treatise on the Treasure of Calculation)

Risalah-Rahat-e-Anfas (Treatise on the Relief of Breath)

Anwarul Qandhar (The Lights of Qandhar)

Copies of these works are available in the Asifiya Library in Hyderabad.

Family and Marital Details:

There are no recorded details about his family. It is believed he married Habeeba Khatun, the daughter of the Nawab of Kurnool. According to "Tahreekush Shifah bin Ausaf e Walajah" by Nawab Amir-ul-Umara (d. 1203 A.H.), Mohammad Akbar is mentioned as Khawja Rahmatullah's brother-in-law, but it is unclear if he married another woman as well. Among his children, only Halima Khatun is mentioned, who was married to Shaikh Makhdoom Abdul Haq Sawi.

Controversy and Spiritual Influence:

Moulana Baqir Agah of Vellore held strong faith in the spirituality of Khawja Rahmatullah. He became enraged when some Shia individuals disparaged Khawja Rahmatullah after his death, which sparked a bitter controversy between Sunnis and Shias from 1207 to 1216 A.H. Agah composed the following chronogram:

"سر اهل يقين وخواجة دين ملاذ و ملجاء

هر سالك راه تنش وابسته حكم شريعت

دلش از هر مقام و حال آگاه ازيں

دار فنا بگذشت و بگذاشت دل احباب

را در درد جانگاه بر آمد از صرير خامه

فرياد بحق گرديد واصل رحمة الله"

"He is the pinnacle of certainty and the refuge of religion,

Every traveler on the path is dependent on the command of the law,

Aware of his heart in every state and situation,

He passed from this fleeting abode and left the hearts of his beloveds

In deep sorrow and lament, cries were heard from every corner,

By God's truth, mercy was attained."

Nawab Muhammad Ali Walajah erected a tomb over his grave in 1204 A.H., as مخدوم indicated by the following chronogram:

"شاه هند امير والا جاه ساخت اين گنبد فلك آسا حاتم محمود بانيش گرديد ابن صاحب درگاه هاتف غيب گفت تاريخش قبه عرش منزلت ناگاه. (١٢٠٤ ه"

From Shaikh Fakhruddin Mehkari Naiti:

"Moulvi Baqir Agah says:

سر عبد حق مخدوم اهل معرفت آنکه بودش نور مطلق در نگاه در بيان كل شي في كل شي كوه را سنجيد در ميزان كاه بعليين كشد پابند جاه گر خيال رفعتش آرد بدل هر كه بينا گشت از ارشاد او ديد در هر ذره صد خورشيد جاه چود ز خود بگذشته شد باقي بحرق تا ابد "(سويش فنا را نيست راه خامه تاريخ وفاتش زد رقم امجد اهل معارف رفته آه (١١٦٦ ه

Chronogram for the Year of Death:

(عمده اهل حقائق رفته آه (١١٦٥ م

Translation:

"The chief among the people of realities has departed. (1165 A.H.)"

This date corresponds to the year of his burial in Madras at the beginning of 1166 A.H.

Shaikh Makhdoom Abdul Haq was well versed in Arabic and Persian and also in Islamic sciences, especially mysticism. The Muslims and Hindus equally respected him. The Hindus called him "gyan bhandari گیان بهنڈاری)‏ " . The learned scholars of the city and other people paid frequent visits to him and were admitted by him into his order. Shaikh Fakhruddin Mehkari Naiti Bekhud (died 1143 A.H.) and Syed Shah Abul Hasan Qurbi (died 1182 A.H) of Vellore became his disciples in the art of mysticism. Both of them have written several qaseedas about him. Shaikh Fakhruddin says :-

Moulvi Baqir Agah says:

سر عبد حق مخدوم اهل معرفت آنكه بودش نور مطلق در نگاه در بيان كل شي في كل شي

كوه را سنجيد در ميزان كاه بعليين كشد پابند جاه گر خيال رفعتش آرد بدل هر كه بينا گشت

از ارشاد او دید در هر ذره صد خورشید جاه چود ز خود بگذشته شد باقی بحرق تا ابد سویش فنا را نیست راه خامه تاریخ وفاتش زد رقم امجد اهل معارف رفته آه ١١٦٦ ه

This date corresponds to the date of his burial in Madras in the beginning of 1166 A.H. He found the chronogram of the year of his death in the following words.

Nawab Muhammad Ali Walajah constructed a tomb over Khawja Rahmatullah's grave in 1204 A.H., as evidenced by the following chronogram:

شاه هند امیر والا جاه ساخت این گنبد فلک آسا حاتم محمود بانیش گردید ابن مخدوم "
"(صاحب درگاه هاتف غیب گفت تاریخش قبه عرش منزلت ناگاه. (١٢٠٤ ه

Translation:

"The chief among the people of realities has departed. (1165 A.H.)"

This corresponds to the year of his burial in Madras at the beginning of 1166 A.H.

Shaikh Makhdoom Abdul Haq was proficient in Arabic, Persian, and Islamic sciences, particularly mysticism. He was equally respected by Muslims and Hindus alike, with Hindus calling him "gyan bhandari". Scholars and visitors frequented him, gaining admission into his order.

His disciples included Shaikh Fakhruddin Mehkari Naiti Bekhud (died 1143 A.H.) and Syed Shah Abul Hasan Qurbi (died 1182 A.H.) of Vellore, both of whom composed numerous qaseedas in his honor.

Translated Poems

From Syed Shah Abul Hasan Qurbi:

"He wrote a lengthy poem titled Jawahir-al-Asrar (Jewels of Secrets), which I extensively quoted in my article on Qurbi. He says:

"The Shaikh among his people is like a prophet among his nation; our elder, praise be to Allah, is the companion of prophets."

"In another poem, Qurbi says:

"Qurbi became a sacrifice at your feet; from disbelief, he became a Muslim. He became both body and soul; from you, Makhdoom, I am intoxicated."

From Muhammad Najeeb, son of Ahmad Ali, author of Karamat-e-Qadriya:

"Welcome, O sky! Your upbringing is the sun, the sea surrounds you with pearls. Your pleasant garment is eternal life; circling your dome is a symbol of greatness. Description of your power, O sacred one, given the creative universe. May your kingship be over the world, chosen for the elite in your court. He revealed all his secrets to your heart, discovered from the mysteries of cosmic and divine existence, found the path."

This was composed by him in 1267 A.H., as these lines indicate:

"He said, 'This story was narrated by Jalil Muhammad Najeeb, son of Ahmad Ali, in the year twelve hundred and sixty-seven, during the second half of Shawwal. It concluded in Madras, achieving fame as Karamat-e-Qadriya.'"

اے بسا اقطاب راجز قرب جاناں وصل نیست جز تو اے واصل کہ دیدے روئے جاناں بے حجاب ہست پردہ در میان قرب و وصل وصل را ہرگز نباشد با تقرب انتساب وصل آن باشد کہ پردہ از میان برخواستن قرب نبود این چنین ای دوست در عالی جناب کس ندانست و نداند ای شہ کشف و شہود پایہ جاہ ترا واللہ اعلم بالصواب ہر کراخواہی بہ بخشی بر ثریا دستگاہ و آن کہ را خواہی زبالا افگنی در زیر آب ہر چہ می خواہی تو از درگاہ خلاق مجید می کنند از غایت لطفش ہمان دم مستجاب ہر تمنائیکہ بودت مختفی اندر دست لطف ایزدی برداشت از رویش نقاب یعنی آن کام دلت ایزد برآورد از کرم وز طفیل ات کام چون ما مستمندان ہم شتاب عالمی از یمن فیضت کام دلہا یافتند دستگیر دو جہانت کرد مستطاب کعبہ دنیا ودینی قبلۂ حاجات خلق رب ضمیر قدوۃ اہل سخان مظہر جود وأواب صاحب علم الیقینی سرور عین الیقین چہرہ حق الیقین دیدی عیان تر از آفتاب تافتہ بر خاطر تو بارہا انوار غیب منکشف سر الہی گشت بر تو بے حساب

Here is the translation of the provided Persian passage:

"O how many are the radiant stars of union, O Beloved! There is no union except with You, O Uniter. Only You, O Uniter, who has seen the face of the Beloved without veil, for the veil between union and proximity is never union; it is affiliation with proximity. Union is that from which the veil is removed. No one, O Friend, in the high assembly knew or knows this secret, O King, the discovery and witnessing. The foundation of your sovereignty, and Allah knows best what is right. Whoever you wish, you elevate to the zenith, and whoever you wish, you immerse in the depths. Whatever you desire, from the court of the Creator Majid, they fulfill immediately, from the extreme of His grace. Every desire hidden in your hands, the divine grace lifted the veil from His face. That aspiration of your heart, God fulfilled through His benevolence, and from your benefaction, the needy like us also hasten. The entire world attained the fulfillment of their desires from the abundance of your grace, O Giver of both worlds. The Kaaba of this world and the religion, the Qibla of the needs of creation, the Lord of the hearts, the model for the people of insight, the manifestation of generosity and the Acceptor of repentance. The possessor of the knowledge of certainty, the leader of the eye of certainty, the manifestation of the truth of certainty. You have seen the reality more clearly than the sun, shining upon your heart multiple times, the mysteries of the unseen revealed, and the divine secret unfolded limitlessly upon you."

This translation captures the essence of the spiritual and mystical praise contained in the Persian passage.

In this chapter Muhammad Najeeb has pointed out that Shaikh Makhdoom Abdul Haq was the author of more than a hundred works. He says:-

يردل چون آفتابت هيچ سر پوشيده نيست علم پيدا و نهان از تو نباشد در حجاب چونکه هستى بحر عرفان و جهان معرفت كرده تصنيف در علم تصوف صد كتاب هر بيان دلكش نغز كتاب خويش را داده تطبيق با شرع رسول مستطاب چون تصانيف تو تصنيفى نكرده هيچ كس هم نگفته هيچ تصنيف ترا لايق جواب ز انكه خود فهميدن سر كلامت مشكل است س چه خواهد گرفت كج فهم جوابش با صواب پس ور بگويد كس كتابت را جواب از ابلهى هرزه و بيهوده باشد جمله گفتارش خراب حق شناسانش بگويند حق نگفت و يا ره گفت ياوه گويان را سزاوار آمده زجر و عقاب گفتن فهميدگان و گفت نافهميدگان همچو قرآن شريف وقول كفار كذاب گفته مخدوم ما را هر كه از پندار و كين ناشمرده رد نمايد گردد او خود رد باب بت شك اى مخدوم عالم جمله تصنيفات تو گشت مقبول خدا ومرسل عالى جناب

Muhammad Najeeb has paid a glowing tribute to Shaikh Makhdoom Abdul Haq Sawi in the following words. He says:-

Muhammad Najeeb has praised Shaikh Makhdoom Abdul Haq Sawi in the following words:

"O heart! Like the sun, there is no hidden secret from you. Knowledge, manifest and hidden, originates from you. In the veil of existence, you are the sea of gnosis, and the world of knowledge has authored a hundred books in the science of Sufism. Each eloquent expression and profound book has provided its own interpretation in accordance with the Shari'ah of the beloved Messenger. Since no one else has authored works like yours, no one has ever spoken of your authorship. This is because understanding the essence of your discourse is complex; what understanding will comprehend its response accurately? Thus, if anyone questions your book, the response would be futile and pointless, as all his words would be in vain. Those who understand and those who do not understand are both deserving of punishment, just like the noble Qur'an and the false statements of disbelievers. If anyone rejects our Makhdoom due to his thoughts and enmity, he himself will become a reject, O Makhdoom of the world! All your compositions have become accepted by Allah, the Exalted, and are revered."

This passage reflects Muhammad Najeeb's deep admiration for Shaikh Makhdoom Abdul Haq Sawi's prolific literary contributions and his spiritual stature.

هر کتابی را که تصنیف از پی نفع همه کرده ای آفتاب جهل سوز علم تاب از نگاه اقدس حضرت رسول دو جهاں بگذرانیدی و شد منظور و مقبولش کتاب چون پسندش کرد ، کردی در جهانش آشکار همچنین جمله تصانیف تو باشد مستجاب چونکه شد ذات جلیل القدر تو دریاي فیض گنجهای بذل را بر روی ما بکشاد وباب اقتباس از نور شمعت ماه و پروین می کنند وز تو علم ارباب معنی می نمایند اکتساب حاجت محتاج در درگاه تو موجود هست کس نرفت از آستانت ناشده مقصود یاب چون نهاده تاج خود بر آستانت آسمان در جهان شد دولت

جاوید باوی همرکاب باز آنکس را کجا حاجت بدیگر اوفتد چونکه شد از آستان فیض بارت
فیضیاب خادمان در گه تو از همه مستغنی اند زان که هستند آن همه در ظل تو چون تو آفتاب
خاص درگاه خداوند حضرت مخدوم ما است هست او خورشید گردون دعا مستجاب بر
غلام خویش گستر لطف خود یا مرشدی مست گردان از عنایت جان اور ابی شراب زانکه
جان ناظران چهره دلدار غیب

Muhammad Najeeb continues to praise Shaikh Makhdoom Abdul Haq Sawi with these words:

"O Sun! Every book that you have authored, aiming for benefit, has become a burning torch of knowledge, dispelling ignorance from the perspective of the holy presence of the Prophet, who transcended both worlds and became accepted and esteemed. Just as your preferred book became apparent in its world, so too shall all your compositions be accepted. For your essence, O majestic being, is like an ocean of grace, bestowing the treasures of generosity upon us. They draw from the light of your candle, moon, and Pleiades, and through you, they demonstrate the knowledge of the lords of meaning. The acquisition of needs by the needy at your doorstep exists, as none have gone from your sanctuary without attaining their goal. When you placed your crown upon your doorstep, it ascended to the heavens in the world, and eternal prosperity became its companion. Where else would someone need to go, once they have received the abundance of your grace? Your servants in your sanctuary are independent from all, as they reside in the shade of you, the special Sun, at the court of the Lord. Our Makhdoom is indeed the sun of the heavens, granting the prayers of his humble servant. Extend your kindness, O guide, and turn us into intoxicated seekers through the grace of your soul and spirit.For the souls of beholders, behold the face of the beloved unseen."

This passage eloquently expresses Muhammad Najeeb's profound admiration and spiritual reverence for Shaikh Makhdoom Abdul Haq Sawi, highlighting his profound influence and spiritual guidance through his vast literary contributions and his enlightened presence.

مست باشد بی شراب و سیر باشد بی کباب اے نجیب از قرب جوئی گردن از طاعت مپیچ
وصل گرمی باید از مخدوم عالم سرمتاب

In another place he has praised him in the following words :-

شه دو جہاں خاص پروردگار براہ خدا کام او استوار چراغ رہ سر سالکان طریق پناه جہان
دستگیر غریق عارفان مرشد کاملان فروزنده چشم روشندلان شهنشاه دوران و قطب مدار
بر اور ننگ معنی شه کامگار پذیرای امرش زمه تا سمك سپهرش غلام است و چاکر ملك
بسالك نمائنده راه راست بلی در جهان ذات مخدوم ما است جهان روشن از پرتو ذات اوست
فلك زیر ظل عنایات او است بشام و سحر رحمت کردگار بقبر شریفش بیادا نثار

The following are some of the works written by him. (1) Mizan-al-Tawheed میزان التوحید pp. 162x15) in Persian giving a mystical inter-pretation of the وحدة الوجود) Unity of Existence). It was printed several times and it was published in 1311 A.H. by Syed Burhanuddin in his Burhania Press, Madras at the instance of Moulvi Mohammad Makhdoom Hussain Sawi, the grandson of Shaikh Makhdoom Sawi.

(2) Miftah-al-Kul Bayan-e-Waqe (4) رسالة اسم الله Risalah-e-Ism-ul-Lah

(3) مفتاح الكل عقائد (Aqaid-e-Sufiya (6) رساله ولايت Risalah-o-Wilayat (5)

رسالة عصای موسی واقع بيان) Asa-e-Musa (8) تجدد امثال Tajaddud-e-Armthal (7)

9(صوفيه) Mizan-al-Maani (10) ميزان المعاني) Risalah-e-Hayat-e-Jan رساله

11(جان حيات) Rasalah-e-Subhan-e-Mureedeen (12) رسالة سبحان مريدين)

Jawami بسط و قبض رسالة Risalah-e-Qabz-e-Bast (13) جوامع الاسرار ul-

Asrar

Muhammad Najeeb continues to extol Shaikh Makhdoom Abdul Haq
Sawi in the following manner:

"Let him be intoxicated without wine and satiated without kebab, O
Najeeb! Seek closeness through worship, do not entangle your neck in
obedience. Warmth of connection is required from the Lord of the
world, from Makhdoom, the pinnacle of knowledge."

In another instance, he praises him with these words:

"O King of both worlds, nurturer of the special ones, the guide on God's
path, his work is steadfast. The lamp on the path for seekers, the refuge
for those drowned in the world, the supporter of the mystics, the perfect
guide, illuminator of clear-hearted visionaries, the sovereign of the age
and the axis of the orbit. Yes, indeed, the essence of our Makhdoom is
in the world, illuminated by the radiance of his essence. The celestial
sphere is under the shade of his kindness, with the dawn and morning
of the Merciful Creator."

He concludes with a heartfelt tribute:

"To his noble tomb, we offer our homage."

These passages illustrate Muhammad Najeeb's profound admiration and reverence for Shaikh Makhdoom Abdul Haq Sawi, depicting him as a spiritual luminary whose teachings and guidance transcend worldly knowledge and lead seekers towards spiritual enlightenment and closeness to God.

Shaikh Makhdoom Abdul Haq infused in his disciples and students, a great spirit for the revival of Islam and checked the rising spirit of Shi'sm in Carnatic. Qurbi says:-

در جهان قطب حق محبوب حق شد پیرما خادمان را نیز در محبوبیت او رهبر است مبتدی صحبتش تلقین ده هر منتهی است زانکه از هر منتهی آن مبتدی دانا تر است مبتدی را می کنند از یك توجه منتهی بردرش هر منتهی مثل رهی و چاکر است

In another place Qurbi writes :-

اگر قدوة المحققین زبدة العارفین شیخ مخدوم القادري قدس سره درین ملك تشریف نیاورده اكثر مردمان این جا در گرداب روافض افتادند.

Among his sons Shah Ghulam Ahmad was a great scholar and mystic. He was born in 1151 A.H., and studied under his father and other

The works attributed to Shaikh Makhdoom Abdul Haq Sawi reflect his deep scholarship and spiritual insights, aimed at both enriching Islamic knowledge and guiding his disciples towards spiritual fulfillment. Here is a continuation of the list of his works:

Dibacha-e-Miftah-al-Tafasir (ديباچه مفتاح التفاسير)

Mafatih-al Ghaib (مفاتيح الغيب)

Ghayat-ul-Tamtheel (غاية التمثيل)

Risala-e-Sama-o-Rag (رساله سماع و راگ)

Zad-al-Talibeen (زاد الطالبين)

Hayat-al-Salikeen (حياة السالكين)

Pun Gun (پنج گنج)

Tanbeeh-al-Arifeen (تنبيه العارفين)

Risalah-e-Nisbati (رسالة نسبتى)

Al-Tareeq-al-Qaweem fi Sirat-al-Mustaqeem (الطريق القويم في صراط المستقيم)

Risalah-e-Istighna (رسالة استغنا)

Risalah-e-Faiz (رساله فيض)

Daleel-e-Muhkam (دليل محكم)

Mehak (محك المدعى المدعى المدعى)

Chaneemat-al-Waqt (غنيمة الوقت)

Shaikh Makhdoom Abdul Haq Sawi's influence extended beyond his literary output; he imbued his followers with a profound dedication to Islam's revival and countered the spread of Shi'ism in the Carnatic region. His teachings emphasized both scholarly pursuits and spiritual practices, fostering a holistic approach to religious education among his disciples.

His son, Shah Ghulam Ahmad, who was born in 1151 A.H., continued his legacy by studying under him and other prominent scholars, thereby carrying forward the tradition of knowledge and spiritual guidance initiated by Shaikh Makhdoom Abdul Haq Sawi.

He composed poems in Persian first under the pen name of Wahdat وحدت and then changed it to Hag. He was also a student of Mir Abdul Ali Uzlat Surati of Hyderabad. But in his book Al-Saheefat- ul-Mursala الصحيفة المرسلة he gives his pen name as Khursheed خورشيد He wrote several works of which two are extant now.

1. Al-Saheefat-ul-Mursala الصحيفة المرسلة pp. 80 x 12) written by him in reply to a request made to him by his elder brother, Hazrath Muhammad Nasiruddin Sawi in the month of Jamadi II 1173 A.H., for a clear interpretation of the mystical ideas of his father. He first wrote

it in the form of a letter and then undertook to explain the same points in detail into two and ten Mursals respectively In several places he has emphasised on the importance of Shareeat and says that the people should strictly adhere to the rules of Shareeat. He says:-

He has clearly pointed شریعت را مقدم دار اکنون طریقت از شریعت نیست بیرون out that the mystics of his days have adopted a very wrong attitude towards Shareeat. He writes :-

و در ملك هندوستان اصل ملت کیش نفس پرستان شده است بر خود تنگ دانسته بی محابا در تقدیم اوامر و تهدیم نواهی کوشند وحسن افعال و اقوال و اعمال چه در امور دنیا یا در معامله دین اختیار خود کنند و از افعال شنیع مانند ریش تراشیدن ورقص فواحشه را بر علانیه دیدن و غیره و از اعمال کریه مثل حقه کشیدن و جامه و دامن دراز و دستار از حد بزرگ پوشیدن و اقوالیکه موجب خود شناسی رنجش دیگران از ان بکنایه منظور باشد گفتن که درین عصر شعار اکثر مشایخ هندوستان شده است دور باشد و توابعان خود را بترك این مراتب ترغیب و تادیب نماید بلکه فرض عین پندارد.

It seems like you're providing further details about Shaikh Makhdoom Abdul Haq Sawi's disciples and their literary contributions, particularly focusing on Shah Ghulam Ahmad. Shah Ghulam Ahmad, born in 1151 A.H., continued the scholarly and spiritual legacy of his father, Shaikh Makhdoom Abdul Haq Sawi. He studied under his father and other eminent scholars, thereby deepening his knowledge and understanding of Islamic teachings and mysticism.

Original Text:

شریعت را مقدم دار اکنون طریقت از شریعت نیست بیرون He has clearly pointed out that the mystics of his days have adopted a very wrong attitude towards Shariat. He writes :-

Translation:

He prioritized Islamic law; now the mystic path is not outside Shareeat. He clearly pointed out that the mystics of his era had adopted a very misguided approach towards Islamic law. He writes:

"In the Indian subcontinent, the essence of the religious community has become idolatrous, considering themselves narrow-mindedly in presenting commands and vilifying disobedience, striving to exercise their own discretion in good deeds, words, and actions, whether in worldly affairs or religious dealings. They engage in shameful acts such as trimming beards, witnessing indecent dances openly, and more. They perform objectionable actions like cheating, wearing excessively long garments and shawls, and making statements that promote self-justification while causing discomfort to others. It is said that in this era, the slogan of many spiritual leaders of India has become far removed (from true guidance), and it is incumbent upon their followers to abandon such practices and instead promote encouragement and discipline as an absolute duty."

He stressed the primacy of Islamic law, asserting that the mystic path does not exist apart from it. He clearly criticized the mystics of his time for adopting a severely misguided approach towards Islamic law. He wrote:

He has also criticised some of the disciples of his father who were giving a wrong interpretation to the ideals of his father. He also condemned certain followers of his father who were distorting his father's teachings.

In "Dark-ul-Idrak" (Understanding of Perception), written in 1179 A.H. during his journey from Masulipatam to Hyderabad in Ramadan, he responded to requests from his father's disciples to clarify contentious interpretations of mystical terms in his father's writings. The treatise is structured into two chapters (Bab) and a concluding section (Khatima). In the conclusion, he vehemently criticizes the misguided practices of the Sufis of his era:

"It is important to note that nowadays, among both disbelievers and Muslims, hardly anyone exists who does not claim expertise in Sufism and regard themselves as perfected guides. Consequently, the esteem for this noble knowledge has diminished rather than flourished. Prominent teachers in this region spend their days openly discussing and eloquently presenting fundamental truths and insights in Persian, Hindi, and Arabic sermons in streets and markets, viewing this as their livelihood. Once evening falls, after concluding their sermons and receiving a few coins as charity, they each return home contemplating their sustenance needs. Those deeply entrenched in this sect consider themselves less devout than even the least devout followers of India's rulers, while not realizing that they themselves embody demonic traits, asserting 'I am your supreme lord' akin to Pharaoh and Nimrod. They mistakenly believe their thrice-daily prostrations validate their divinity, striving for knowledge they do not fully possess and elevating other forms of knowledge above that imparted by the Teacher of the Kingdom, thus fueling the trade in faith."

Shaikh Ghulam Ahmad Sawi died in 1217 A.H.

His brother Muhammad Muhyuddin was also a great scholar. He wrote a book in Arabic entitled "Minhaj-ul-Muhaqqiqeen" منهاج المحققين. It consists of 284 pages, each page having 12 lines, and is divided into an introduction (muqaddima) and three sections (magalats) and a conclusion (khatima).

Introduction on the basics.

First section on proving monotheism between the Creator and creation with textual evidence.

Second section on proving real difference between the Creator and creation with rational and textual evidence.

Third section on proving unity and differentiation.

Conclusion on the benefits attained by the possessor of this knowledge and explaining what reaches the higher ranks and levels of sciences, knowledge, actions, and others.

This book was completed by him in the month of Rabius Sani in the year 1181 A.H. He was also a poet in Arabic. He composed poems in praise of his father in Arabic, and we find him quoting some of his verses in this book. He wrote many short treatises like "Sawal-o-Jawab" سوال وجواب, "Risalah-e-Istighna" رسالة استغناء, "Miftahul Ghuyub" مفتاح الغيوب, etc. The date of his death is not known. His brothers Ghulam Mahmood and Nasiruddin Sawi were also well versed in Arabic and Persian. Ghulam Ahmad writes about his brother Ghulam Mahmood:

"Praise be to Allah, today in the field of Sufism and following the guidance of the revered mentor, there is no one like my brothers."

Asadullah was succeeded by Shaikh Muhammad Usman Sawi, son of Muhammad Asadullah, who later became the spiritual guide. Shaikh Muhammad Usman Sawi passed away in Udayagiri, Nellore, on the 14th of Zul Qada, 1292 A.H. Muhammad Najeeb praised Shah Usman Sawi in the following words:

نکاتیکه از مو است باریك تر شکافد به تیغ زبان سر بسر کسی را نیست پیشش طاقت گفت دل است از هیبت او سخت خاشع که او هست از خدا بسیار خائف داش در وقت طاقت خوب خاضع

"The points he finely divided through intimate proximity, no one has the strength to utter them head to head with the sword of his tongue.

44

His heart is deeply devout due to his awe-inspiring presence, as he is greatly fearful of God and remains obediently submissive at all times."

Moulvi Muhammad Mahdi Wasif (1217-1290 A.H.)

Moulvi Muhammad Mahdi Wasif (1217-1290 AH) was the son of Moulvi Muhammad Arifuddin Khan Rawnaq, who in turn was the son of Muhammad Ma'ruf from Burhanpur. His family was recognized as descendants of Hazrat Abu Bakr Sıddıq. His grandfather, Muhammad Ma'ruf, moved to Madras during the time of Nawab Muhammad Ali Walajah. A collection of his letters to Asim Khan Mubariz Jung, Umdatul Umara, and others is preserved under the title Insha-e-Maruf (انشاه معروف) in the Madrasa-e-Muhammadi Library, Diwan Saheb Bagh, Madras.

Arifuddin Khan Rawnaq was born in 1192 AH and studied Arabic and Persian under Moulvi Muhammad Ismail, Moulvi Haji Muhammad Muqeem, Moulvi Ghulam Mohyuddin Mujiz, and Moulana Moulvi Baqir Agah. At twenty, he became a teacher and tutor to Tajul Umara Ali Husain Khan Majid. He learned modern Persian idioms from Mirza Muhammad Sadiq Shirazi Kawkab, who came to Madras in 1217 AH and passed away in 1219 AH. Following Nawab Umdatul Umara's death in 1216 AH, he served in Cuddapah, Bellary, and Chittoor. He also worked for a time in the office of Sir Thomas Munro, Governor of Madras (1820-1827).

Before 1259 AH, Rawnaq traveled to Hyderabad seeking suitable employment but eventually returned to Madras. In 1266 AH, he was admitted to the poetic assembly by Nawab Ghulam Ghouse Khan Bahadur, recommended by Afzalush Shuara Muhammad Husain Khan Raqim. He was known for his ability to compose poems extemporaneously. Nawab Ghulam Ghouse Khan wrote

در انواع سخن قدرت تامه می داشت و هریکی بکمال خوبی می نگاشت بارها در محافل کثیره شعر بدیهی می گفت و گوهر سخن بمثقب قلم شتابی رقم می سفت

In various forms of speech, he possessed complete eloquence, and each word he wrote was adorned with perfection. He often recited extemporaneous poetry in numerous gatherings, swiftly inscribing the essence of his words with his skilled pen.

Due to old age, his mental capacity weakened, affecting his ability to write. Nawab Saheb noted

اکنون بسبب پیرانه سری وضعف بدنی اختلال بدماغش جا گرفته و آن طاقت یکقلم از دستش بیرون رفته پای در دامن عزلت و یذکر الهي شغل ورزیده

Now, due to old age and physical weakness, his mind has become disturbed, and he has lost the ability to write as he once did. He has retired into seclusion, dedicating himself to divine remembrance.

Rawnaq passed away in Madras on 25th Zul Qada 1270 AH. He composed many short and long poems, some of which have been included in various anthologies. His diwan (a collection of poems, pp. 114) was published in Hyderabad by his great-grandson Moulvi Abdul Basith. He also wrote a qaseedah (a form of Persian poetry) titled Wasf-e-Jashn-e-Azeem (وصف جشن عظیم) consisting of 67 lines, in praise of Nawab Azeemjah when he became a regent after the death of his brother Nawab Azam Jah in 1241 AH. It begins with the following verses

عروس طالع ایام جلوه آراشد که در حدیقه گیتی گل طرب واشد

به هر طرف که نظر رفت طرفه سرسبزی است

چو گازمین سخن شهر و دشت خضراشد

بفکر قطعه رباعی غزل قصیده در آ

اگر هوای سخن در سرت مهیا شد

چو این نوید بگوش دام رسید بوجد

دماغ شاعریم نیز خامه فرسا شد

بوصف جشن عظیمی غزل سرا گشتم

که قفل کارفرو بسته است این واشد

The bride of fortunate times adorned herself with beauty, causing the flower of joy to bloom in the garden of the world. Everywhere one looks, there is marvelous greenery, as if the fields and city have become verdant with eloquence. If the desire for poetry arises in your mind, come and create verses, couplets, and odes. When this news reached my ears, my poetic fervor was rekindled, and I began composing verses in praise of this great celebration, as if a lock had been opened.

He concludes the qaseedah with the following lines

بفن نظم نموده است گرچه عمری صرف

زدست جورفاك جمله محو و منسی شد

ز چند سال گرفتار بے معاشی ها است

محقر نظر اقربا احیا شد

زعهد شاه شهادت پناه استحقاق

مللی را درین ریاست فیاض

والدش راشد بها

علي قدامتش متحقق زچار پشت

و ليك قلنا بكم نصيبی دور از حضور والا شد

Although I have spent my life in the art of poetry, I have been erased and forgotten due to the tyranny of time. For many years, I have been caught in the trap of poverty, and the respect of relatives has been revived. During the era of the noble king, he deservedly held this position with generosity, his father, Rashid, and Ali's ancient honor verified from four generations. However, we say, our share is distant from the exalted presence.

بفیض صحبت جد تو گشته چرن ممتاز

همیشه محترز کار و بار ادنی شد

چوب صله نشد از درگهت سخن سنجی

بر آستانه نو عرض بنده بر جاشد

بصد ادب کنم از آرزوی خویش رقم

ز عمرها بسرم این خیال پیدا شد

Through the grace of your grandfather's company, I have become distinguished, always avoiding trivial matters. When no reward came from your court for my poetry, I humbly presented myself anew at your threshold. With utmost respect, I inscribe my wish, a thought that has been with me for years.

باوستادی شهزاده سرفرازم کن

که در ضمیر من خسته این تمنا شد

بفارسی کتب نظم و نثر دارم بهر

گهر شناس خریدار عمده کالا شد

By standing by me, O Prince, you will honor me, for this desire has settled in my weary heart. I have books of poetry and prose in Persian, valuable items for a connoisseur of gems.

ز قدرور تبه و آداب صحبت امرا

مرا سلیقه رفیض حضور اعلی شد

شدایی مراد تو رونق قبول در گاهش

کف دعاے تو پردر از آرزوها شد

From my experiences with nobles and the etiquette of their company, I have gained a refined taste for the presence of the exalted. By achieving your favor, I have found acceptance and my prayers are filled with aspirations.

همیشه تا چمن دهر از سحاب کرم

باغبانی دستت که بس مطرا شد

خجسته ماند و گیتی شود ثنا خوانت

دعای بنده درگاه این مودی شد

که باد ظل تو پاینده بر مفارق خلق

توئی که آهن و روی از گفت مطلا شد.

May the garden of the world always be nourished by the cloud of your generosity, tended by your blessed hand. May you remain prosperous and the world sing your praises. This is the prayer of your devoted servant, that your shadow may always protect the people. You are the one whose words turn iron and copper into gold.

شد این قصیده مسمی بوصف جشن عظیم

لا قلة هزار شور و شغب زان بسطح غبرا شد

This qaseedah is named 'Wasf-e-Jashn-e-Azeem,' and it brought about a thousand cheers and excitement.

Moulvi Muhammad Mahdi Wasif (1217-1290 AH) was the son of Moulvi Muhammad Arifuddin Khan Rawnaq, who in turn was the son of Muhammad Ma'ruf from Burhanpur. His family was recognized as descendants of Hazrat Abu Bakr Sıddıq. His grandfather, Muhammad Ma'ruf, moved to Madras during the time of Nawab Muhammad Ali Walajah. A collection of his letters to Asim Khan Mubariz Jung, Umdatul Umara, and others is preserved under the title Insha-e-Maruf (انشاه معروف) in the Madrasa-e-Muhammadi Library, Diwan Saheb Bagh, Madras.

Arifuddin Khan Rawnaq was born in 1192 AH and studied Arabic and Persian under Moulvi Muhammad Ismail, Moulvi Haji Muhammad Muqeem, Moulvi Ghulam Mohyuddin Mujiz, and Moulana Moulvi Baqir Agah. At twenty, he became a teacher and tutor to Tajul Umara Ali Husain Khan Majid. He learned modern Persian idioms from Mirza Muhammad Sadiq Shirazi Kawkab, who came to Madras in 1217 AH and passed away in 1219 AH. Following Nawab Umdatul Umara's death in 1216 AH, he served in Cuddapah, Bellary, and Chittoor. He also worked for a time in the office of Sir Thomas Munro, Governor of Madras (1820-1827).

Before 1259 AH, Rawnaq traveled to Hyderabad seeking suitable employment but eventually returned to Madras. In 1266 AH, he was admitted to the poetic assembly by Nawab Ghulam Ghouse Khan Bahadur, recommended by Afzalush Shuara Muhammad Husain Khan Raqim. He was known for his ability to compose poems extemporaneously. Nawab Ghulam Ghouse Khan wrote

در انواع سخن قدرت تامه می داشت و هریکی بکمال خوبی می نگاشت بارها در محافل
کثیره شعر بدیهی می گفت و گوهر سخن بمثقب قلم شتابی رقم می سفت

In various forms of speech, he possessed complete eloquence, and each word he wrote was adorned with perfection. He often recited extemporaneous poetry in numerous gatherings, swiftly inscribing the essence of his words with his skilled pen.

Due to old age, his mental capacity weakened, affecting his ability to write. Nawab Saheb noted

اکنون بسبب پیرانه سری و ضعف بدنی اختلال بدماغش جا گرفته و آن طاقت یکقلم از دستش
بیرون رفته پای در دامن عزلت و یذکر الهي شغل ورزیده

Now, due to old age and physical weakness, his mind has become disturbed, and he has lost the ability to write as he once did. He has retired into seclusion, dedicating himself to divine remembrance.

Rawnaq passed away in Madras on 25th Zul Qada 1270 AH. He composed many short and long poems, some of which have been included in various anthologies. His diwan (a collection of poems, pp. 114) was published in Hyderabad by his great-grandson Moulvi Abdul Basith. He also wrote a qaseedah (a form of Persian poetry) titled Wasf-e-Jashn-e-Azeem (وصف جشن عظیم) consisting of 67 lines, in praise of Nawab Azeemjah when he became a regent after the death of his brother Nawab Azam Jah in 1241 AH. It begins with the following verses

عروس طالع ایام جلوه آراشد که در حدیقه گیتی گل طرب واشد

به هر طرف که نظر رفت طرفه سرسبزی است

چو گازمین سخن شهر و دشت خضراشد

بفکر قطعه رباعی غزل قصیده در آ

اگر هوای سخن در سرت مهیا شد

چو این نوید بگوش دام رسید بوجد

دماغ شاعریم نیز خامه فرسا شد

بوصف جشن عظیمی غزل سرا گشتم

که قفل کا رفرو بسته است این واشد

The bride of fortunate times adorned herself with beauty, causing the flower of joy to bloom in the garden of the world. Everywhere one looks, there is marvelous greenery, as if the fields and city have become verdant with eloquence. If the desire for poetry arises in your mind, come and create verses, couplets, and odes. When this news reached my ears, my poetic fervor was rekindled, and I began composing verses in praise of this great celebration, as if a lock had been opened.

He concludes the qaseedah with the following lines

بفن نظم نموده است گرچه عمری صرف

زدست جورفاك جمله محو و منسی شد

ز چند سال گرفتار بے معاشی ها است

محقر نظر اقربا احیا شد

زعهد شاه شهادت پناه استحقاق

مللی را درین ریاست فیاض

والدش راشد بها

علي قدامتش متحقق زچار پشت

و لیك قلنا بكم نصیبی دور از حضور والا شد

Although I have spent my life in the art of poetry, I have been erased and forgotten due to the tyranny of time. For many years, I have been caught in the trap of poverty, and the respect of relatives has been revived. During the era of the noble king, he deservedly held this position with generosity, his father, Rashid, and Ali's ancient honor verified from four generations. However, we say, our share is distant from the exalted presence.

بفیض صحبت جد تو گشته چرن ممتاز

همیشه محترز کار و بار ادنی شد

چوب صله نشد از درگهت سخن سنجی

بر آستانه نو عرض بنده بر جاشد

بصد ادب کنم از آرزوی خویش رقم

ز عمرها بسرم این خیال پیدا شد

Through the grace of your grandfather's company, I have become distinguished, always avoiding trivial matters. When no reward came from your court for my poetry, I humbly presented myself anew at your threshold. With utmost respect, I inscribe my wish, a thought that has been with me for years.

باوستادی شهزاده سرفرازم کن

که در ضمیر من خسته این تمنا شد

بفارسی کتب نظم و نثر دارم بهر

گهر شناس خریدار عمده کالا شد

By standing by me, O Prince, you will honor me, for this desire has settled in my weary heart. I have books of poetry and prose in Persian, valuable items for a connoisseur of gems.

قدرور تبه و آداب صحبت امرا

مرا سلیقه رفیض حضور اعلی شد

شدایی مراد تو رونق قبول در گاهش

کف دعاے تو پردر از آرزوها شد

ز

From my experiences with nobles and the etiquette of their company, I have gained a refined taste for the presence of the exalted. By achieving your favor, I have found acceptance and my prayers are filled with aspirations.

همیشه تا چمن دهر از سحاب کرم

باغبانی دستت که بس مطرا شد

خجسته ماند و گیتی شود ثنا خوانت

دعای بنده درگاه این مودی شد

که باد ظل تو پاینده بر مفارق خلق

توئی که آهن و روی از گفت مطلا شد.

May the garden of the world always be nourished by the cloud of your generosity, tended by your blessed hand. May you remain prosperous and the world sing your praises. This is the prayer of your devoted servant, that your shadow may always protect the people. You are the one whose words turn iron and copper into gold.

شد این قصیده مسمی بوصف جشن عظیم

لا قلة هزار شور و شغب زان بسطح غبرا شد

This qaseedah is named 'Wasf-e-Jashn-e-Azeem,' and it brought about a thousand cheers and excitement.

Moulvi Muhammad Mahdi Wasif (1217-1290 AH) received his education in Persian from his father Rawnaq and uncle Shaikh Mueenuddin Siddiqui. He studied Arabic under several scholars, including Syed Abdul Qadir Husaini (d. 26th Shawwal 1257 AH),

Moulvi Mufti Abdur Rahman (d. 10th Safar 1297 AH), Shaikh Muhammad Alam (d. 26th Rabi II 1255 AH), Moulvi Yousuf Ali Khan (d. 5th Jamadi I 1281 AH), Qazi Badruddowlah, and his elder brother Moulvi Abdul Wahab Madarul Umara Bahadur. He also learned English.

Wasif lived in Cuddapah, Bellary, and Chittoor with his father for a while. At seventeen, he moved to Madras around 1234 AH, where he taught Arabic and Persian to the employees of the East India Company for seventeen years. During his time in Madras, he visited Natharnagar and Trichnopoly and became a student and disciple of Moulvi Syed Jame Alam, a preacher and spiritual guide, son of Qadre Alam and grandson of Moulvi Badr-e-Alam. He joined a poetic assembly started by Nawab Ghulam Ghouse Bahadur and frequently critiqued the works of his contemporaries. He had strained relations with Afzalush Shuara Moulvi Muhammad Husain Khan Raqim and others, whom he criticized for their attitudes towards him.

In Safar 1271 AH, Wasif moved to Hyderabad and became a teacher at Darul Uloom, established by Nawab Salarjung in 1270 AH. He passed away on 30th Rajab 1290 AH (23rd September 1873 AD). Wasif was proficient in Arabic, Persian, and Urdu, and left behind several works in these languages. Some of his notable works in Arabic include

Tahzib-al-Akhlaq (تهذيب الاخلاق) A translation of selected chapters from Akhlaq-e-Muhsini by Mulla Husain Kashifi, printed at Mazharul Ajaib Press, Madras, in 1278 AH.

Hadeeqat-ul-Maram (حديقة المرام) This book contains life sketches of scholars from Madras and Hyderabad, printed at Mazharul Ajaib Press, Madras, and published in 1279 AH.

Firasat-ul-Insan fi Nasath-al-Luqman (فراسة الانسان في نصائح اللقمان) An Arabic translation of a Persian book by Muhammad Azam Ali Khan Bahadur, containing stories of Luqman. When he went to Hyderabad in Safar 1271 AH, he began working on this translation.

Moulvi Muhammad Mahdi Wasif stayed with his friend Muhammad Azam Ali Khan Bahadur in Hyderabad. There, Bahadur showed him a Persian book he had written, titled Al-Nasaih-al Luqmaniya (النصائح اللقمانية), and requested Wasif to translate it into Arabic, in which Wasif was more proficient. Wasif agreed to this request and translated the book. He wrote

بقدر لغات المرء يكثر نفعه و تلك له عند الشدائد اعوان فبادر الى حفظ اللغات مسارعا فكل لسان في الحقيقة انسان

The more languages a person knows, the more beneficial they become, aiding them in times of need. Therefore, hasten to learn languages quickly, for every tongue is, in truth, a person.

He presented a copy of this book to Moulvi Abdul Wahab Madarul Umara in 1274 AH.

Here are some other works by Wasif in Arabic;

Tahzib-al-Akhlaq (تهذيب الاخلاق) A translation of selected chapters from Akhlaq-e-Muhsini by Mulla Husain Kashifi, printed at Mazharul Ajaib Press, Madras, in 1278 AH.

Hadeeqat-ul-Maram (حديقة المرام) This book contains life sketches of scholars from Madras and Hyderabad, printed at Mazharul Ajaib Press, Madras, and published in 1279 AH.

Firasat-ul-Insan fi Nasath-al-Luqman (فراسة الانسان في نصائح اللقمان) An Arabic translation of a Persian book by Muhammad Azam Ali Khan Bahadur, containing stories of Luqman. Wasif began this translation when he went to Hyderabad in Safar 1271 AH.

Lulu-e-Manthur Adab-i-Ziyarat-il-Qabur (لؤلؤے منثور في آداب زيارة القبور) A 14-page book on the etiquette of visiting graves, printed and published by Mazharul Ajaib Press, Madras, on 17th Jamadi I 1278 AH.

Matalib-al-Furqan (مطالب الفرقان) An index of the Quran, 44 pages long, published by Mazharul Ajaib Press, Madras, in 1281 AH.

Persian

Ma'dan-al-Jawahir (معدن الجواهر) An anthology of Persian poets, written in 1260 AH, comprising 522 pages.

Daleel-e-Sate (دلیل ساطع) A dictionary of Urdu, Hindi, and other words explained in Persian, compiled in 1248 AH, printed at Mazharul Ajaib Press, Madras, in 1266 AH, and published by Syed Abdul Lateef Altaf on 6th Jamadi I 1277 AH.

Hikayat-e-Dilpasand (حکایات دلپسند) This book contains 216 stories translated into Persian from English, originally translated from Greek. Compiled in Shaban-Ramadhan 1253 AH, Wasif wrote in the preface

نظر بتعمیم فائده اش من هیچمدان ژولیده بیان که واصف ارباب کمالم از زبان اهل فرنگ بلسان اهل عجم درآوردم

For the benefit of the readers, I, a humble and poor writer, have translated these stories from the language of the Franks into the language of Persia, making them accessible to the people of culture and refinement.

Moulvi Muhammad Mahdi Wasif continued his literary contributions with several notable works. Here are some of his additional writings:

Zakheerat-ul-Uqba fi Sharh-e-Asma Illahil Husna ذخيرة العقبى في شرح
اسماء الله الحسنى) pp. 120 x 17). It was published in 1275 A.H. by
Mazharul Ajaib Press, Madras.

Waseelat-al-Najat وسيلة النجات) pp. 104 × 15). explaining the ninety nine
names and epithets of the Prophet. It was published in 1275 A.H.

Husn-e-Khitab wa Radd-e-Jawab 24) حسن خطاب ورد جواب) short tract
regarding 37 allegations levelled against him by Afzalush Shuara
Moulvi Muhammad Husain Khan Raqim. It was written by him on 27th
Jamadi 1 1287 and published in the same year.

It seems that Wasif presented a copy of his memoirs Madan al Jawahir
to Shirin Sukhan Khan Raqim and asked him to delete the three or four
folios written by Wasif about Shaikh Nasir Ali Sirhindi. But Raqim
remarked that he (Wasif) was an elderly person more experienced in
Persian language. Then instead of deleting the portion from Madan al
Jawahir by himself, he bitterly criticised Wasif in a tract under the name
of جواب اعتراضات واصف to which Wasif refers and says-

بنده نوازا چون در سير باغ در مجلس مشاعره برهنمائی مولانا حاجی مولوی محمد حسين
راقم افضل الشعرا با هديه سنيه معدن الجواهر شرف ملازمت دريافتم، آيا عرض نكردم كه
امروز اين كتاب و مولف آن مملوك سركار اند ، بنظر اصلاح ملاحظه فرموده هر چه در

باب شیخ ناصر علی مرحوم سقیم و مذموم معلوم میشود آن را از کتاب من برآرند و برین بنده منت نهند، آیا نه فرمودید که تو به نسبت من کهن سالی و مهارت تو در لسان فارسی ظاهر است من بعد از مائدة الوان نعمت سرکار با دیگر ملازمین که حاضر بودند بهره ور شدم، پس از رفع فتنه یعنی چاك کردن سه چهار ورق اعراض کرده در رفع اعتراضات و هتك حرمت واصف کوشیدن آیا بجای خویش بود . که پرورده کشتن نه مردی بود دستم از پی داد. سردی بود!

بنده نوازا چون در سیر باغ در مجلس مشاعره برهنمائی مولانا حاجی مولوی محمد حسین راقم افضل الشعرا با هدیه سنیه معدن الجواهر شرف ملازمت دریافتم، آیا عرض نکردم که امروز این کتاب و مولف آن مملوك سرکار اند ، بنظر اصلاح ملاحظه فرموده هر چه در باب شیخ ناصر علی مرحوم سقیم و مذموم معلوم میشود آن را از کتاب من برآرند و برین بنده منت نهند، آیا نه فرمودید که تو به نسبت من کهن سالی و مهارت تو در لسان فارسی ظاهر است من بعد از مائدة الوان نعمت سرکار با دیگر ملازمین که حاضر بودند بهره ور شدم، پس از رفع فتنه یعنی چاك کردن سه چهار ورق اعراض کرده در رفع اعتراضات و هتك حرمت واصف کوشیدن آیا بجای خویش بود. که پرورده کشتن نه مردی بود دستم از پی داد. سردی بود!

O kind sir, during our conversation in the garden and at the poetic assembly where Moulana Haji Moulvi Muhammad Husain Raqim, Afzalush Shuara, was present, you bestowed the honor upon me by accepting the gift of Madan al Jawahir. Did I not request that this book and its author are at your service, and that you kindly review it and remove anything found defective or blameworthy about Shaikh Nasir Ali Did you not respond that I am older and more proficient in Persian than you After benefiting from the lavish hospitality provided by you and in the company of other attendees, I refrained from deleting the three or four pages myself. Was it proper to respond to this by criticizing me and attacking my honor It is not manly to destroy what one has nurtured. Seeking justice for my grievances was indeed a cold comfort!

Wasif's works are preserved in various libraries and reflect his proficiency in Arabic, Persian, and Urdu, contributing significantly to the literary and scholarly heritage of his time.

Wasif held Tajul Umara Ali Hussain Khan Majid in high regard, expressing his admiration in his writings

اگر تاج الامرا ابن عمدة الأمرا ابن والاجاه مرحوم همه كليات صائب را با معان نظر مطالعه كردندى بمدد طبع روشن و ذهن رسا اعظم النصحا شدند

If Tajul Umara, son of Umdatul Umara, son of the late Walajah, had studied all the works of Saib with an insightful mind, assisted by a bright nature and clear intellect, he would have become the greatest of advisors. (From Khatima Husn Khitab wa Radd-e-Jawab)

Abdul Kareem Wala, Wasif's son, composed the following chronogram

آن مولوى مهدى واصف تخلصش كو هست در كمال فضيلت مآب نيك تاليف كرد نسخه چو درج جواهرى چون سلك در سطور بصد آب و تاب نيك شخصى كه رد شعر على رد نموده بود در رد آن دوباره نمود اكتساب نيك هم منشيان وهم شعرا حرزجان كنند مملو است از

صنايع نادر كتاب نيك تاريخ ختم نسخه چو والا سروش گفت حسن خطاب نادر ورد جواب
نيك ١٢٨٧ ه

That Moulvi Mahdi Wasif, whose pen name is well known for his virtuous excellence, composed a manuscript like a jeweled case, as beautiful as a string of pearls in lines. The person who had refuted poetry of Ali refuted it again, earning good praise. Both the clerks and the poets guard their lives, and the book is filled with rare crafts. The date of completion, as said by exalted Sarosh, is the year 1287 AH.

Sharait-i-Talluqadari (شرائط تعلقدارى) This 16-page pamphlet discusses the expected behavior of Talluqadars (landowners) towards their subjects. It was printed and published in 1277 AH.

Abwab-al-Nasaih (ابواب النصائح) Copied by Muhammad Abdul Kareem, dated 17th Safar 1276 AH.

Diwan-e-Wasif (ديوان واصف) A collection of his Persian poems, printed and published twice—first on 15th Zulhaj 1264 AH from Muhammadi Press, Madras, and again in 1278 AH.

These works and reflections highlight Wasif's literary contributions and the high esteem in which he held his contemporaries, alongside his own poetic and scholarly achievements.

Wasif expressed his views in these lines

نمودم قبله بینائی آن حسن خدائی را

خبر دادم زلطف صورتش اسباب معنی را

تهی از باده الفت مبادا جام دل یارب

که نبود آبرو در انجمن مینائی خالی را

بحیرت بود موسی همچنان دروادی ایمن

فتادن بر زمین حل کرد رمز لن ترانی را

بمحفل گریه شادی است اکنون گریه مینا

بموج باده یکسر داده ام سامان تقوی را

بهای دل توان سیر گلستان سخن کردن

توان چیدن بدست فکر گلهای معانی را

مرا نزدیك خود جاده غمم افزون

اگر خواهی که باشد بی قراری بیشتر در آب ماهی را

شده واصف زبس ممتاز اندر موشگافی ها

زبیت ابرویش برخواند دیوان هلالی را

I made the beauty of the divine my guide,

And informed of the grace of his form, the means of meaning.

O Lord, may the cup of the heart never be devoid of the wine of affection,

For it loses its prestige in an empty crystal gathering.

Moses remained in awe in the valley of security,

Falling to the ground, he solved the mystery of 'You will never see me.'

Now, in the assembly, weeping is joy, as tears are precious,

In the wave of wine, I have completely surrendered my piety.

One can enjoy the garden of words by valuing the heart,

One can pick the flowers of meaning with the hand of thought.

Keep me close if you want my sorrow to increase,

If you wish for more restlessness in the water for the fish.

Wasif has become distinguished in his subtleties,

Reading the Diwan of Hilali from the arc of her eyebrow.

Urdu

Rawza-e-Rizwan (روضه رضوان) This 196-page collection of Urdu poems, praising Imam Husain, was printed in 1275 AH at Azeemul Akhbar Press, Madras by Ghulam Husain, in the college. Wasif used the pen name Miskeen in his Urdu compositions.

مسکیں مجھت پیری میں ھوی مدح کی خواہش

بی شك ھي یہ فیضان مرے بخت جوان کا

کس مرشد کونین کا یہ فیض ھے یارو

مسکین کے دیوان میں عرفان کو دیکھا

In my old age, Miskeen desires praise,

Surely, it is the blessing of my youthful fortune.

O friends, whose guidance is this grace,

In Miskeen's Diwan, enlightenment is seen.

These excerpts and poems illustrate Wasif's literary prowess and the depth of his admiration for his contemporaries and spiritual figures, along with his own contributions to Persian and Urdu literature.

Persian

میں صورت شبیر میں قرآن کو دیکھا

ریحان میں سب روضہ رضوان کو دیکھا

مسکین کے دیوان کی جب سیر کریں احباب

انصاف سے فرماویں کیا روضہ رضوان ھے

In the form of night, I saw the Quran,

In the fragrance of basil, I saw all the gardens of paradise.

When friends tour Miskeen's Diwan,

Tell them with justice, what is Rawza-e-Rizwan

Urdu

دشت بلا میں نقشہ ہی اك لالہ زار کا داغ سیاہ جس کا ہے گردہ بہار کا

مسکیں تو اپنے نقص سخن کا کر اعتراف نقصان بھی علاج ہے عین الکمال کا

In the desert of adversity, there is a mark of a tulip garden,

A black stain which is the mark of the spring's orbit.

Miskeen, acknowledge the flaws in your speech,

For admitting faults is indeed the remedy for perfection.

Chronogram by Kashif

کرد تصنیف روضہ رضواں حضرت واصفم بطرز شگفت از سر یادگار کاشف سال نو نہال غم امام بگفت

Kashif composed Rawza-e-Rizwan in a surprising manner,

In memory, Imam revealed the seeds of sorrow in the New Year.

Minhaj-al-Alleen An Urdu translation of Kimiya-e-Saadat by Imam Ghazali, printed and published by Azeezi Press, Madras.

Tahseenul Akhlaq A book on moral improvement.

Shia'arul Muttaqeen Divided into four chapters on clothing, jewelry, headgear, and veils. Compiled in Hyderabad in 1272 AH and printed at Azeemul Akhbar Press, Madras in 1274 AH.

Khulasat-al Takmeel

Matlub-al-Atibba: An Urdu translation of Mujiz-al-Tib on Greek medicine.

Diwan-e-Miskeen A collection of poems by Miskeen, published by Mazharul Ajaib Press, Madras in 1278 AH.

Imla Nama-e-Wasif In its introduction, Wasif mentions:

"Readers should be aware that learning the correct spelling of words is essential. Due to its limited practice among energetic youth, I, Wasif, have provided a useful resource for learning in a few pages used in lines and prose, naming it Imla Nama-e-Wasifi. Their learning is plentiful. If Imla Nama is of interest, expert reading is also a work of art in the field of word and meaning."

This book was printed and published from Azizia Press, Madras in Jamadi Ist 1267 AH.

Wasif's sons, Hakeem Abdul Basith Sahib Isha, Moulvi Abdur Rahman, and Muhammad Abdul Kareem, were also eminent scholars and poets in Persian and Urdu. Ishq was born in 1238 AH and studied Arabic and Persian under his uncle Haji Zainul Abideen and Nawab Khan-e-Alam Khan Bahadur. He also pursued medicine and obtained a diploma from the Medical College, Madras. After residing in Mysore, he settled in Hyderabad post-1279 AH and lived there until his passing on 5th Rabi I 1302 AH. His diwan in Persian and Urdu, titled Tarana-e Ishq, was published by his grandson Moulvi Abdul Basith, son of Mulla Qayyum, in 1359 AH.

Other members of this family were also distinguished scholars. Mullah Abdul Qayyum, son of Hakeem Abdul Basith Ishq, left a mark in history through his dedicated service to the country and the nation. Born in 1270 AH, he passed away on 9th Ramadhan 1324 AH. Mulla Abdul Qayyum states

The speech that is the pride of the world is mine, born of my house. The homeland retains the poetry of my springs.

Gulzar-e-Hamd, published by Sultan al Waizeen Sultan Mahmood Hanafi from Mazhar-al-Ajaib Press, Madras, contains two panegyric poems in Persian and a few verses in Urdu composed by Khushnood. One of the three poems is quoted below

How delightful are the eyes that behold the countenance of Mustafa!

Oh, fortunate is the body that has turned into the dust of Mustafa's courtyard.

O Khizr, you never tasted the water of life if you did not sip from the drops of Mustafa's ablution water.

I roam every direction and ask every being, 'Where can I lose myself in the quest of Mustafa'

I wander aimlessly like a madman, entranced by his mention and his name.

My soul is tethered to the strand of Mustafa's blessed hair.

How can I describe the praise of that pure essence

I make my own words sing the praise of Mustafa.

With contentment, rise like the sun on the day of resurrection,

May my face turn towards Mecca in prayer from every direction.

O Lord, grant me the fortune to recite these verses in Yathrib,

These verses of mine, drawn towards Mustafa.

Conclusion

Shaikh Makhdoom Abdul Haq Sawi and Moulvi Muhammad Mahdi Wasif represent pillars of knowledge, spirituality, and literary excellence in the 19th century South Asian landscape. Each of these figures, through their distinct contributions, enriches our understanding of scholarship, religious discourse, and cultural heritage.

Shaikh Makhdoom Abdul Haq Sawi's profound impact as a Sufi saint and scholar is evident in his teachings and spiritual guidance, which continue to resonate through generations. His emphasis on inner purification and devotion to Allah remains a guiding light for spiritual seekers.

Moulvi Muhammad Mahdi Wasif, a polymath proficient in Arabic, Persian, and Urdu languages, stands out for his literary contributions and educational endeavors. His works, ranging from poetry to educational treatises, exemplify his dedication to intellectual pursuits and cultural preservation amidst the changing dynamics of colonial India.

Collectively, these two personalities embody a commitment to knowledge, spirituality, and cultural heritage that transcends their era. Their lives and works serve as a testament to the enduring significance of Islamic scholarship and literary excellence in shaping societal values and intellectual discourse in South Asia.

In commemorating Shaikh Makhdoom Abdul Haq Sawi and Moulvi Muhammad Mahdi Wasif, this study celebrates their profound legacies and invites reflection on their contributions to the rich tapestry of Islamic intellectual tradition and cultural heritage in the region.

Bibliography

S. Diwan, *Vellore Puratchiyil Veeramigu Muslimgal 1806 (the Valliant muslims in Vellore Mutiny in 1806),* India:Sukhaina Publishers, 2012.

H. A. R Gibb, *Travels of Ibn Battuta* .New Delhi: Goodword Books, 2011.

S. Nainar Mohammed Husayn, *Saidakkadiru Marakkayar Tirumana Vazhttu,* Madras: Sultana Abdullah Publishers, 1953.

Samuel John, Ed. *Tamil as a classical Language,* Chennai: Institute of Asian Studies, 2010.

Tayka Shuaib, *Arabic, Arwi and Persian in Sarandib and Tamil Nadu,* Madras: Imamul Arus Trust, 1993.

P. T. Srinivas Iyengar, *History of the Tamils from the Earliest Times to 600 A.D,* Madras: C Coomaraswamy Naidu & Sons, 1929.

K.M.A. Ahamed Zubair, *Islamic Mysticism in Tamil Nadu,* Saarbrucken: LAP Lambert Academic Publishing, 2017.

K.M.A. Ahamed Zubair, "Usrathus Shaik Sadaqathullah Appa wa Khidmathuhaa al-deeniyya wal Ilmiyya".PhD diss., University of Madras, 2003.

Buy your books fast and straightforward online - at one of world's fastest growing online book stores! Environmentally sound due to Print-on-Demand technologies.

Buy your books online at
www.morebooks.shop

Kaufen Sie Ihre Bücher schnell und unkompliziert online – auf einer der am schnellsten wachsenden Buchhandelsplattformen weltweit! Dank Print-On-Demand umwelt- und ressourcenschonend produzi ert.

Bücher schneller online kaufen
www.morebooks.shop

MIX
Papier aus verantwortungsvollen Quellen
Paper from responsible sources
FSC® C105338
FSC
www.fsc.org

Printed by Books on Demand GmbH, Norderstedt / Germany